# low-fat

igloo

# igloo

Published by Igloo Books Ltd
Cottage Farm
Sywell
NN6 0BJ
www.igloo-books.com

10 9 8 7 6 5 4 3 2 1

ISBN: 978 1 84817 638 6

Project Managed by R&R Publications Marketing Pty Ltd

Food Photography: R&R Photostudio (www.rrphotostudio.com.au)
Recipe Development: R&R Test Kitchen

Front cover photograph © Stockfood/Antje Plewinski

Printed and manufactured in China

# contents

# introduction

Our health is affected by what we eat in all sorts of ways and there are some ailments that may require a special diet. This section only gives a general overview of healthy eating. If you have any specific concerns about your health, talk to your doctor.

## What's in Food?

### CARBOHYDRATES

We need carbohydrates for energy – it really is our daily fuel. Carbohydrates should make up a little more than half our daily calorie intake. Most of it should come from starchy foods like cereals, breads, pasta and potatoes, which are known as complex carbohydrates. These foods supply a steady stream of energy as well as useful vitamins and minerals.

Sugar is an example of a simple carbohydrate, which provides a quick energy boost but no nutrients. Fruits contain natural sugars, and also supply important vitamins and minerals.

### PROTEINS

Every cell in the body – from fingernails to bones and muscles – needs protein for growth, maintenance and repair. Proteins are made up of compounds called amino acids. Anyone who eats a varied diet automatically supplies their body with all the amino acids and protein it needs. But because meat, fish and dairy products are such rich sources of protein, vegetarians and vegans need to ensure they eat a good variety of vegetables, grains, nuts and pulses to meet their daily requirements.

### FATS

If we didn't have fat in our diet, our bodies wouldn't function properly. In fact, to be healthy, up to a third of all the calories we eat should come from fats. Unfortunately, many of us have a higher proportion of fat than this in our diet, and a high-fat diet can lead to obesity and an increased risk of heart disease and other illnesses.

Saturated fats, such as those found in animal fats, are most likely to increase the risk of heart disease by raising blood cholesterol levels. Fatty meats and full-fat dairy products are the main source of saturates in our diets. You don't have to avoid burgers, sausages, cheese, butter and cream completely, just choose lower-fat versions where you can. Buy lean meat and semi-skimmed milk, for example, or just spread your butter a bit more thinly and have a smaller dollop of cream instead!

**THE OTHER FATS IN OUR DIET**

Polyunsaturates and monounsaturates – may actually help to lower blood cholesterol. Remember, it's your whole diet that counts. Liquid vegetable oils such as sunflower, grapeseed and olive oil are all high in unsaturated fats. Oil-rich fish such as mackerel, sardines and salmon contain a particular type of polyunsaturated fat (Omega 3) which is also important for a healthy heart. Try to eat oil-rich fish twice a week.

Except for those people who have inherited high cholesterol levels, cholesterol can usually be lowered quite effectively through diet – largely by cutting down on saturated fats and boosting the intake of soluble fibre. Because it binds with cholesterol, soluble fibre helps your body get rid of it as waste, together with undigested fibre. Fruit, vegetables, wholemeal bread, oats and pulses are all good sources of soluble fibre.

**SALT**

People who eat too much salt are more likely to suffer from high blood pressure. In turn, high blood pressure is a risk factor for heart disease and stroke. The recommended daily intake of salt is 5g (about 1 teaspoon), however, the typical person has about 10g. Salt is made up of chlorine and sodium. If you are concerned about your sodium intake, check the nutrition information on food labels.

## Eating a Balanced Diet

A balanced diet is one that supplies just the right amount of energy and nutrients for your body's needs. Your body can compensate for times when you eat more or less than usual, but in the long term, your diet will be directly reflected by your health.

Eating a healthy, balanced diet not only makes you feel good, it also helps you maintain the right weight for your height and reduces your risk of heart disease and many other ailments. It's now also thought that diet is linked to a third of all cancers. But it's important to remember that no matter how healthy someone's diet may be, there can never be an absolute guarantee they will not get some form of cancer or heart disease.

The easiest way to have a healthy diet is to ensure it's varied. It may help to imagine a large plate with all the food you eat in a day arranged on it. About a third should be filled with complex carbohydrates (bread, potatoes, rice, and pasta). Another third should be filled with a good variety of fruit and vegetables – fresh, frozen or canned, at least five servings a day. Just under a sixth of the plate should be filled with meat, fish, poultry, nuts or pulses. The same amount should be taken up by dairy foods, such as cheese, milk and yogurt (try to choose lower fat alternatives when you can). This leaves a thin portion for fatty and sugary foods like cakes, chips, soft drinks, and oils. Of course you may not have all these foods during the day.

Some foods are thought to be more protective than others, especially for certain cancers. Foods which contain antioxidants are beta carotene (the plant form of Vitamin A), Vitamin C and Vitamin E (see the Vitamins and minerals information on pages 8–9 for the best sources.) Using the nutritional information on food and drink labels will also help you achieve a healthy diet. Simply adding up the amount of fat you eat each day will help you keep the balance right

– but try to keep an eye on the sodium and sugar too. Check your intake against these guideline daily amounts, which are for men and women of average weight and physical activity:

| Each Day | Men | Women |
| --- | --- | --- |
| Fat | 95g | 70g |
| Calories | 2,500 | 2,000 |
| Sugars | 70g | 50g |
| Sodium | 2½g | 2g |

## Water, Drinks and Alcohol

Water is essential for life. Adults need 2–3 litres of water a day. However, some ways of drinking it are healthier than others.

Soft drinks can contain a lot of sugar and should be drunk sparingly. You shouldn't drink excessive amounts of coffee or tea either as they both contain the stimulant caffeine, which can lead to insomnia and headaches.

Like most things, alcohol is fine as long as you don't overdo it. A couple of glasses of wine with a meal may actually help to reduce the risk of heart disease, but much more than three or four glasses has the reverse effect. A man can have three to four units a day and a woman can have two to three, but not every day and it does depend on your size. A unit is one glass of wine, a half pint of medium strength lager or beer or one measure of spirits. If you do have too much to drink, try to steer clear of alcohol for the next couple of days to give your body chance to recover.

## Fertility and Pregnancy

Research shows that the chances of having a healthy pregnancy are significantly increased by eating healthily for at least three months before the baby is even conceived. Women should also take folic acid supplements until 12 weeks into their pregnancy, which greatly reduce the chances of the baby being born with spina bifida. Both men and women should limit their alcohol consumption – excessive amounts are linked to lower fertility and birth defects.

There is no need to eat much more than normal during pregnancy – an intake of about 2,400 calories should be adequate. Some additional nutrients are needed though: zinc for the baby's growth and sexual development and iron to treat or prevent anaemia. An extra serving of bread, cereal, pasta or some other complex carbohydrate is advised, together with the equivalent of a pint of milk to meet extra calcium and protein requirements.

Foods to avoid include liver, as it is very high in vitamin A and too much of it can harm the baby. Blue or soft cheeses, such as Camembert and Brie, and other unpasteurised foods such as patés should also be avoided, as there is a small risk of them being infected by a bacterium called listeria. Eggs, meat, fish and any ready-prepared meals should all be cooked thoroughly to avoid other forms of food poisoning. Alcohol should be limited to the occasional glass of wine, but try to avoid it altogether during the first 12 weeks of pregnancy.

## Children

Rapid growth means children need proportionately more nutrients than adults. However, because their stomachs are smaller than adults', they need smaller and more regular meals. Young children should not be given low-fat foods, such as skimmed milk – they need the extra calories of the full-fat versions. They can have low-fat foods once they're five years old and eating a varied diet.

Developing good eating habits in children early will mean they are more likely to eat healthily as they grow up. Try to get children used to the natural flavours of fresh fruit and vegetables, but don't force them to eat foods they don't like. Teeth are at greatest risk of decay during childhood, so avoid giving them too many sugary foods and drinks.

## Being the Right Weight

If you're overweight, you're certainly not alone. However, the seriously overweight run a higher risk of high blood pressure, heart disease and cancer, than people of normal weight.

Following a healthy balanced diet within specific calorie guidelines is the best way to lose weight permanently. Women should aim for between 1,900–2,500 calories a day, depending on how active they are, while men need 2,500–3,000 calories. For a sensible weight loss of around 900g a week, aim for a reduction of 400 calories per day. Eat plenty of fruit, vegetables, and complex carbohydrates and cut down on things which are full of empty calories, like sweets, soft drinks, and alcohol. Avoid fatty foods and grill rather than fry things whenever you can.

Crash-dieting seldom works and all too often its results are short-lived. Fad diets are often dangerous, as they don't provide your body with the full range of nutrients it needs to function properly. The best way to reach or maintain a healthy weight is diet combined with exercise. Introduce exercise gradually and take advice from a doctor if you haven't exercised for a long time. If you do succumb to the odd treat, don't let it upset your long-term goal.

## Being a Healthy Vegetarian

If you eat a good variety of dairy products, grains, vegetables, cereals and pulses, your diet will supply all the protein you need and be lower in saturated fat and include more fibre than the typical meat eater's. However, meat is the richest source of several key nutrients and vegetarians and vegans should take extra care to ensure they're getting enough iron, Vitamin B12, calcium and folate. Beans, lentils, dark leafy vegetables and wholegrain cereals provide iron; fortified breakfast cereals and dairy products are good sources of Vitamin B12; soya products, milk, cheese, yogurt and dark leafy vegetables supply calcium and most green leafy vegetables, peanuts, fortified breakfast cereals, and yeast extract are rich in folate. Iron deficiency is a common problem among women, especially vegans and vegetarians, in which case supplements may be necessary.

# soups,
# starters
# and salads

# Salade Niçoise

(see photograph on page 10)

4 small waxy potatoes

2 cups fine green beans

3 medium eggs

4 tomatoes

12 white onions, thinly sliced

170g can tuna in oil, drained

8 black olives, halved

6 anchovy fillets (optional), halved

2 small lettuce leaves, separated

watercress sprigs to garnish

## DRESSING

4 tablespoon sunflower oil or olive oil

1 tablespoon white wine vinegar

salt and black pepper

## SALAD

1  Boil the potatoes in a saucepan of salted water for 15–20 minutes, until tender. Drain and set aside until cool enough to handle, then dice. Meanwhile, cook the beans in another saucepan of boiling salted water for 5 minutes or until tender. Drain and halve.

2  Put the eggs into a saucepan of cold water. Bring to the boil, then cook for 10 minutes. Peel the eggs under cold running water and cut into quarters lengthways. Place the tomatoes in a bowl and cover with boiling water. Leave for 30 seconds, then peel and cut into wedges.

3  Place the potatoes, beans, eggs, tomatoes, onions, tuna, olives, and anchovies (if using) in a large bowl.

## DRESSING

1  Mix together the dressing ingredients, pour over the salad and toss lightly. Line a platter with the lettuce leaves and spoon the salad on top. Garnish with the watercress.

### Serves 4

*Note: No wonder Salade Niçoise has become so popular – it's colourful, healthy, and delicious.*

# Cumin-Spiced Carrot Soup

(see photograph opposite)

1 tablespoon olive oil

1 large onion, chopped

1 clove garlic, crushed

3 sticks celery, chopped

1 tablespoon ground cumin

750g carrots, thinly sliced

4 cups vegetable stock

black pepper

fresh coriander to garnish

1  Heat the oil in a large saucepan. Add the onion, garlic, and celery and fry gently for 5 minutes or until softened, stirring occasionally. Add the cumin and fry, stirring, for 1 minute to release its flavour.

2  Add the carrots, stock and pepper to the onion mixture and stir to combine. Bring to the boil and simmer, covered, for 30–35 minutes, until the vegetables are tender, stirring occasionally.

3  Remove the pan from the heat and cool for a few minutes. Purée the soup until smooth in a food processor, liquidiser, or with a hand blender. Return to a clean pan and reheat gently. Serve garnished with the fresh coriander.

### Serves 4

*Note: This thick soup, will really warm you up on a cold winter's night. To get the best flavour, spend a bit extra on fresh stock. Serve with naan bread.*

# Thai Fish Sticks with Cucumber Salad

## FISH STICKS

4 spring onions, chopped

small handful of fresh coriander

500g cod loin or other skinless white fish fillet, cubed

3 tablespoons Thai red curry paste

1 teaspoon salt

2 teaspoons lime juice

1 large egg white

12 stalks lemongrass

## SALAD

½ cucumber, peeled and very thinly sliced

4 tablespoons white wine vinegar

4 tablespoons white sugar

1 large red or green chilli, deseeded and chopped

1 small spring onion, sliced

4 tablespoons cold water

## SALAD

1   Combine the cucumber, vinegar, sugar, chilli, spring onion and cold water. Cover and leave in a cool place until needed.

## FISH STICKS

1   Blend the spring onions and coriander in a food processor until finely chopped. Add the fish, curry paste, salt and lime juice and blend until the fish is finely chopped. Add the egg white and continue blending until the mixture is stiff.

2   Divide the fish mixture into 12 portions, then carefully press each around a lemongrass stalk, forming a 'sausage' shape. Preheat the grill to high. Place the fish sticks on a lightly oiled baking sheet, then grill for 6 minutes, turning once, until cooked and lightly browned on all sides. Serve with the cucumber salad.

### Serves 4

*Note: Cooking these spicy kebabs on lemongrass sticks gives them a lovely citrus flavour. The simple salad combines slivers of cool cucumber with a little red-hot chilli.*

# Thai Hot and Sour Prawn Soup

2 stalks lemongrass

375g whole raw shell-on prawns, defrosted if frozen

1 tablespoon vegetable oil

4 cups chicken stock

1 clove garlic, crushed

25mm piece fresh root ginger, chopped

grated zest of 1 lime and juice of 2 limes

1 green chilli, deseeded and finely chopped

salt and black pepper

1 tablespoon Thai fish sauce (nam pla)

1 red chilli, deseeded and sliced, and 2 tablespoon chopped fresh coriander to garnish

1   Peel the outer layers from the lemongrass stalks and chop the lower white bulbous parts into 3 pieces, discarding the fibrous tops. Shell the prawns, leaving the tails attached and reserving the shells for the stock. Cut a slit along the back of each prawn with a sharp knife and remove the black vein. Rinse the prawns, then refrigerate until needed.

2   Heat the oil in a large saucepan. Fry the prawn shells for 2–3 minutes, until pink. Add the stock, garlic, ginger, lemongrass, lime zest, green chilli and salt to taste. Bring to the boil, then reduce the heat, cover and simmer for 20 minutes.

3   Strain the stock and return to the pan. Stir in the fish sauce and lime juice and bring to the boil. Add the prawns, reduce the heat and simmer for 3 minutes, or until the prawns turn pink and are cooked through. Season with pepper and serve garnished with the red chilli and coriander.

### Serves 4

Note: This popular Thai soup, known as Tom Yum Kung, will set the taste buds tingling. It has a wonderfully fragrant citrus flavour, followed by a real chilli kick.

# Pikelets with Smoked Salmon and Horseradish

(see photograph opposite)

½ cup crème fraîche

1 tablespoon creamed horseradish

1 tablespoon chopped fresh dill, plus extra to garnish

squeeze of fresh lemon juice

1 teaspoon clear honey

salt and black pepper

8 pikelets

250g smoked salmon slices

1 Preheat the grill to high. In a bowl, combine the crème fraîche, horseradish, dill, lemon juice and honey, then season with salt and pepper.

2 Toast the pikelets under the grill for 1–2 minutes, until golden, then turn them over and cook for a further 1–2 minutes. Top each pikelet with a spoonful of the crème fraîche mixture, some smoked salmon and a sprinkling of pepper. Serve garnished with the dill.

**Serves 4**

*Note: Pikelets are small batter pancakes similar to Russian blinis. Their texture makes them perfect partners for smoked salmon and creamy horseradish.*

# Vegetable Toasts with Tomato Dressing

2 courgettes, thinly sliced lengthways

2 carrots, thinly sliced lengthways

2 red peppers, deseeded and thinly sliced

sea salt and freshly ground black pepper

4 thick slices white bread

1 tablespoon sunflower oil

## DRESSING

2 tomatoes

4 tablespoon virgin olive oil

2 spring onions, sliced

1 tablespoon white wine vinegar

1. Place the courgettes, carrots and peppers in a bowl and season well. You can use a vegetable peeler to make long ribbons with zucchini and carrots.

2. Toast the bread for 3 minutes each side or until golden brown.

3. Heat the sunflower oil in a large frying pan over a high heat and cook the vegetables for 4 minutes, stirring all the time, until they've softened and are just tender. Remove and set aside.

## DRESSING

1. Place the tomatoes, in a bowl of boiling water for 30 seconds, then peel, deseed and finely chop. In the same pan, heat the olive oil, and add the spring onions and vinegar. Cook, stirring occasionally, for 1–2 minutes, until hot, then stir in the tomatoes. Pile the vegetables on top of the toasts, drizzle with the hot dressing and serve.

### Serves 4

*Note: The dressing, drizzled over the pan-fried vegetables, soaks into the crispy toast, making a stunning dinner party starter. Smaller versions make fabulous canapés. Beta carotene is the antioxidant and pigment found in many great-tasting brightly coloured vegetables. Tomatoes get their colour from a different but particularly potent antioxidant pigment called lycopene.*

# Chef's Autumn Salad

salt and black pepper

250g broccoli, cut into small florets

1 romaine lettuce, leaves torn

1 red onion, halved and sliced

12 cucumbers, peeled and diced

2 sticks celery, sliced

2 carrots, cut into matchsticks

2 apples, diced

250g wafer-thin cooked turkey or
ham slices

2 tablespoons each raisins and roasted
salted peanuts, chopped (optional)

## DRESSING

1 teaspoon Dijon mustard

juice of ½ lime

⅝ cup low-fat plain yoghurt

2 tablespoons olive oil

1 tablespoon chopped fresh coriander

## DRESSING

1   Mix together the mustard, lime juice, yoghurt, oil and coriander.

2   Place the lettuce, onion, cucumbers, broccoli, celery, carrots, and apples in a large bowl. Pour over the dressing and toss to coat. Arrange the turkey and ham slices in the centre of a shallow serving dish or platter and spoon the salad around the edge. Scatter over the raisins and peanuts (if using).

## SALAD

1   Bring a large saucepan of salted water to the boil. Add the broccoli, return to the boil, then cook for 1–2 minutes, until slightly softened. Drain and leave to cool for 15 minutes.

Serves 4

Note: Chef's Salad can have almost anything in it. This one makes good use of colourful fresh vegetables and apples and comes with a zingy lime and coriander dressing.

# Roasted Vegetable Salad

3 red onions, quartered

3 potatoes, scrubbed and cut into wedges

2 courgettes, thickly sliced

2 yellow peppers deseeded and thickly sliced

4 tomatoes, halved

2 tablespoons olive oil

sea salt and freshly ground black pepper

Parmesan cheese shavings (optional)

## DRESSING

3 tablespoons extra virgin olive oil

2 tablespoons clear honey

1 tablespoon balsamic vinegar

finely grated zest and juice of ½ lemon

## SALAD

1 Preheat the oven to 200°C. Place all the vegetables in a shallow roasting tin, drizzle over the olive oil and season. Shake the tray gently to coat the vegetables well with oil and seasoning. Bake for about 35 minutes, until the vegetables are very tender and slightly charred at the edges.

## DRESSING

1 Mix all the dressing ingredients together and pour over the roasted vegetables. Toss well and divide onto 4 plates. Top with Parmesan (if using).

Serves 4

*Note: This salad combines a healthy mix of the antioxidant vitamins A, C, and E, plus loads of minerals from the great-tasting vegetables. Remember, the more brightly-coloured the vegetables, the more nutrients they're likely to contain. Roasting brings out vegetables' flavour and intensifies their natural sweetness. Serve with plenty of fresh, crusty bread to soak up the yummy dressing.*

# Thai-Style Shellfish and Pomelo Salad

1 pomelo or 2 pink grapefruit

250g cooked peeled prawns

170g can crabmeat in brine, drained

1 small lettuce, chopped

1 spring onion, finely chopped

**DRESSING**

1 tablespoon groundnut oil

1 clove garlic, finely chopped

1 spring onion, finely chopped

1 red chilli, deseeded and finely chopped

2 tablespoons Thai fish sauce (nam pla)

2 tablespoons dark brown sugar

juice of 1 lime

**DRESSING**

1  First make the dressing. Heat the oil in a small frying pan. Fry the garlic, spring onion, and chilli for 3 minutes or until the garlic has turned pale gold and the spring onion has softened. In bowl, mix together the fish sauce, sugar and lime juice, stir in the spring onion mixture, then set aside for 5 minutes to cool.

**SALAD**

1  Using a sharp knife, slice off the top and bottom of the pomelo or grapefruit, then remove the skin and pith, following the curve of the fruit. Cut between the membranes to release the segments.

2  Mix the pomelo or grapefruit segments with the prawns, crabmeat and lettuce. Pour over the dressing and toss, then sprinkle over the spring onion.

Serves 4

*Note: Pomelos look like grapefruit but have a sweeter flesh. If you can't get them, use pink grapefruit which goes just as well with the crab and prawns in this fresh, light salad.*

# Grilled Vegetable Bruschetta

1 red or yellow peppers, deseeded and
  sliced into strips

1 courgettes, halved and thinly sliced
  lengthways

1 red onion, thinly sliced

2 large plum tomatoes, thickly sliced

3 tablespoons extra virgin olive oil

2 teaspoons wholegrain mustard

freshly ground black pepper

1 ciabatta loaf, cut into 8 slices, or
  8 slices from a baguette

1 clove garlic, halved

8 black olives, pitted and thinly sliced

fresh basil to garnish

1  Preheat the grill to high and line the grill rack with foil. Place the pepper, courgettes, onion and tomatoes in a bowl. Whisk together ⅔ of oil, the mustard and the black pepper, then pour over the vegetables and toss gently to coat.

2  Spread the vegetables in a single layer on the grill rack and grill for 3–4 minutes on each side, until lightly browned. Set aside and keep warm.

3  Toast the bread slices on both sides under the grill and, while still hot, rub the garlic halves over one side of each piece of toast. Divide the vegetables between the toast slices, piling them onto the garlicky sides. Scatter over the olives and drizzle over the remaining oil. Garnish with the fresh basil and serve.

**Serves 4–6**

*Note: This Mediterranean snack is great for drinks parties. Rubbing garlic over the toast gives it a sweet taste that sets off the flavour of the grilled vegetables.*

# Watercress Soup

1 tablespoon sunflower oil

4 spring onions, finely chopped

1 leek, thinly sliced

250g potatoes, diced

1 cup watercress, chopped

2 cups vegetable stock

2 cups semi-skimmed milk

black pepper, coarsely ground

1  Heat the oil in a large saucepan, then add the spring onions and leek and cook gently for 5 minutes or until softened, stirring occasionally. Add the potatoes and watercress to the green onion mixture and cook for a further 3 minutes or until the watercress wilts, stirring occasionally.

2  Stir in the stock, milk and pepper. Bring to a boil, then reduce the heat and simmer, covered, for 20 minutes or until the potatoes are cooked and tender, stirring occasionally.

3  Remove the pan from the heat and cool for a few minutes. Purée the soup until smooth in a food processor, liquidiser, or with a hand blender. Return to a clean pan and reheat gently, until piping hot. Serve seasoned with the black pepper.

**Serves 4**

*Note: This quick soup is full of goodness but it looks and tastes sophisticated enough to serve at any dinner party. For a change, use chopped spinach instead of watercress.*

# Curried Lentil Soup

2 tablespoons vegetable oil

1 onion, chopped

2 teaspoons curry powder

½ teaspoon ground cumin

1 tablespoon tomato pureé

1½ litres vegetable stock

125g red or green lentils

1 small head broccoli, broken into florets

2 carrots, chopped

1 parsnip, chopped

1 stalk celery, chopped

freshly ground black pepper

1 tablespoon chopped fresh parsley

1 Heat oil in a large saucepan, add onion, curry powder and cumin and cook, stirring occasionally, for 4–5 minutes or until onion is soft. Stir in tomato pureé and stock and bring to the boil. Reduce heat, add lentils, cover and simmer for 30 minutes.

2 Add broccoli, carrots, parsnip and celery and cook, covered, for 30 minutes longer or until vegetables are tender. Season to taste with black pepper. Just prior to serving, stir in parsley.

**Serves 6**

*Note: This thick and hearty soup can be made ahead of time and makes a great main meal.*

# Chicken Waldorf Salad

250g cooked boneless chicken breast,
  skinned and diced

4 sticks celery, thinly sliced

1 cup walnuts, roughly chopped

1 green and 1 red-skinned eating apple

juice of ½ lemon

250g mixed salad leaves

snipped fresh chives to garnish

**DRESSING**

4 tablespoons reduced-fat mayonnaise

4 tablespoons low-fat plain yoghurt

½ teaspoon finely grated lemon zest

freshly ground black pepper

1  Place the chicken in a bowl, add the celery and walnuts and stir to mix.
   Core, then dice the apples and toss them in the lemon juice to stop them
   browning. Add to the chicken and mix well.

2  To make the dressing, mix together the mayonnaise, yoghurt, lemon zest, and
   pepper in a small bowl. Then spoon the dressing over the chicken mixture
   and toss lightly to mix. Cover and refrigerate for at least 1 hour before
   serving.

3  To serve, arrange the salad leaves on serving plates and spoon the chicken
   mixture over. Garnish with the fresh chives.

Serves 4

*Note: With its fresh lemony dressing, this simple Waldorf salad makes a
great starter. To turn it into a deliciously light main course just serve it with
some warm crusty bread.*

# Marinated Mushrooms on a Bed of Leaves

4 cups mixed mushrooms, such as shiitake, large open, button and oyster, thickly sliced

250g baby spinach leaves

30g watercress, thick stems discarded

fresh thyme to garnish

**DRESSING**

3 tablespoons extra virgin olive oil

2 tablespoons unsweetened apple juice

2 teaspoons tarragon white wine vinegar

2 teaspoons Dijon mustard

1 clove garlic, crushed

1 tablespoon mixed chopped fresh herbs, such as oregano, thyme, chives, basil and parsley

freshly ground black pepper

**DRESSING**

1  Place the oil, apple juice, vinegar, mustard, garlic, herbs and pepper in a bowl and whisk with a fork to mix thoroughly.

**MUSHROOMS**

1  Pour the dressing over the mushrooms and stir well. Cover and place in the fridge for 2 hours.

2  Arrange the spinach and watercress on serving plates. Spoon the mushrooms and a little of the dressing over the top and toss lightly to mix. Garnish with the fresh thyme.

Serves 4

*Note: Leave the mushrooms to absorb the flavours of the tangy mustard dressing, then pile them onto the spinach and watercress. Warm ciabatta goes well with this salad.*

# Mixed Mushrooms on Herbed Muffins

500g mixed mushrooms, including wild, oyster and shiitake

2 tablespoons olive oil

salt and black pepper

2 tablespoons butter

1 clove garlic, crushed

3 tablespoons chopped fresh parsley

3 tablespoons finely snipped chives, plus extra whole chives to garnish

2 teaspoons sherry vinegar or balsamic vinegar

4 tablespoons low-fat soft cheese

3 English white muffins

1 Halve any large mushrooms. Heat 2 teaspoons of the oil in a heavy-based frying pan, then add all the mushrooms, season lightly, and fry over a medium to high heat for 5 minutes or until they start to release their juices.

2 Remove the mushrooms, drain on kitchen towels, then set aside. Add the rest of the oil and ½ the butter to the pan and heat until the butter melts. Add the garlic and stir for 1 minute.

3 Return the mushrooms to the pan, then increase the heat to high and fry for 5 minutes or until they're tender and starting to crisp. Stir in the remaining butter and 2 tablespoons each of the parsley and snipped chives, drizzle with the vinegar and season.

4 Mix the cheese with the remaining parsley and snipped chives. Split and toast the muffins. Spread the soft cheese mixture over the muffin halves and place on serving plates. Top with the mushrooms and garnish with the whole chives.

**Serves 6**

*Note: Fresh mushrooms have a short shelf life of only 2–3 days and need to be stored in an open container in the refrigerator. Plastic containers should never be used since they retain moisture. Best to use the original container or a paper bag.*

# Plum Tomato, Lentil and Basil Soup

6 tablespoons continental lentils

1 kg plum tomatoes

1 tablespoon olive oil

2 onions, chopped

2 tablespoon sun-dried tomato purée

3 cups vegetable stock

1 bay leaf

black pepper

3 tablespoons chopped fresh basil, plus extra leaves to garnish

1. Rinse the lentils, drain, then add them to a large saucepan of boiling water. Simmer, covered, for 25 minutes or until tender. Drain, rinse and set aside.

2. Meanwhile, place the tomatoes in a bowl, cover with boiling water, leave for 30 seconds, then drain. Remove the skins, deseed and chop. Heat the oil in a large saucepan, add the onions and cook for 10 minutes or until softened, stirring occasionally. Stir in the tomatoes, tomato purée, stock, bay leaf, and pepper. Bring to the boil and simmer, covered, stirring occasionally, for 25 minutes or until all the vegetables are cooked.

3. Remove the pan from the heat and cool for a few minutes. Remove and discard the bay leaf, then purée the soup until smooth in a food processor, liquidiser, or with a hand blender. Return to a clean pan, stir in the lentils and chopped basil, then reheat gently. Serve garnished with the fresh basil.

**Serves 4**

# Chicken and Vegetable Soup

2 rashers bacon

1 onion

2 cloves garlic

1 tablespoon oil

300g can butter beans

1 litre chicken stock

2 potatoes

200g skinless, boneless chicken pieces

1 cup shelled broad beans

freshly ground black pepper

1  Derind bacon and chop into thin strips. Peel onion and chop finely. Crush, peel and chop garlic.

2  Heat oil in a large saucepan and sauté onion, garlic and bacon for 5 minutes or until onion is clear. Drain beans and add to saucepan with stock. Bring to the boil. Peel potatoes and cut into 1cm cubes. Add to stock and cook for 10 minutes.

3  Cut chicken into small pieces if large. Add chicken and broad beans to saucepan. Cook for 5 minutes or until chicken is cooked. Serve hot with freshly ground black pepper.

**Serves 4**

Note: A substantial soup filled with chicken, something starchy like potatoes, rice or pasta, and plenty of vegetables makes a complete meal in a bowl. This is very yummy for a lighter-style winter meal.

# Warm Duck and Mango Salad

1 ripe mango

250g mixed dark salad leaves, such as baby spinach, lollo rosso, and rocket

1 cup sugar snap peas, chopped

4 spring onions, sliced diagonally

2 teaspoon sesame oil

250g boneless duck breast, skinned and cut into strips

fresh coriander to garnish

## DRESSING

3 tablespoons extra virgin olive oil

juice of ½ lime

1 teaspoon clear honey

2 tablespoons chopped fresh coriander

freshly ground black pepper

## SALAD

1 Slice off the 2 fat sides of the mango close to the stone. Cut a criss-cross pattern across the flesh (but not the skin) of each side with a sharp knife. Push the skin inside out to expose the flesh and cut the cubes off. Place in a salad bowl with the salad leaves, peas, and spring onions, then toss together gently to mix.

## DRESSING

1 Whisk together the olive oil, lime juice, honey, coriander and pepper in a small bowl until thoroughly mixed.

2 Heat the sesame oil in a wok or large frying pan, add the duck and stir-fry over a high heat for 4–5 minutes until tender. Add the warm duck to the mango salad, drizzle over the dressing, then toss together to mix. Garnish with the fresh coriander.

Serves 4

# Melon and Grapefruit Salad

1 medium or 2 small melons, such as galia, charentais, honeydew, rockmelon or ogen

2 pink grapefruit

8 tablespoons unsweetened fresh orange juice

1 tablespoon orange liqueur, such as Cointreau or medium sherry (optional)

fresh mint to garnish

1 Cut the melon into segments and remove the seeds. Dice the flesh, or scoop it out using a melon baller. Place in a serving bowl.

2 Slice the top and bottom off each grapefruit and place on a work surface. Using a small serrated knife, cut off the skin and pith, following the curve of the fruit. Holding the grapefruit over a bowl, cut between the membranes to release the segments. Add the segments and juice to the melon.

3 Pour the orange juice and alcohol (if using) over the fruit and stir gently to mix. Cover and refrigerate for at least 1 hour before serving. Garnish with the fresh mint.

**Serves 4**

*Note: If you want a light and refreshing starter, this is it. A dash of liqueur brings out the sweetness of the fruit. If you feel like it, add a few slices of parma ham.*

# meat and poultry

# Lamb Osso Buco

(see photograph on page 34)

2 tablespoons plain flour

salt and black pepper

4 lamb leg shanks, trimmed of
   excess fat

2 tablespoons olive oil

1 onion, finely chopped

1 carrot, finely chopped

1 stick celery, chopped

2 cups canned chopped tomatoes with
   garlic and herbs

1 tablespoon sun-dried tomato purée

¾ cup dry white wine

2 cups lamb stock

**GARNISH**

1 tablespoon chopped fresh parsley

1 tablespoon chopped fresh mint

finely grated zest of 1 lemon

1 clove garlic, finely chopped

**LAMB**

1   Preheat the oven to 160°C. Mix together the flour, salt and pepper on a plate. Dip lamb pieces into the mixture to coat well. Heat 1 tablespoon of oil in large heavy-based frying pan until hot, but not smoking. Add the coated lamb and cook over a medium to high heat for 5–8 minutes, turning frequently, until browned on all sides. Transfer to a deep ovenproof dish.

2   Heat the remaining oil in the pan, add the onion, carrot and celery and cook over a low heat for 4–5 minutes, until softened. Add the tomatoes, tomato purée, wine and stock and bring to the boil, stirring occasionally. Pour over the lamb, cover with foil and bake for 1¾–2 hours, until the meat is tender, turning it over halfway through. Season to taste.

**GARNISH**

1   Mix together the parsley, mint, lemon zest, and garlic. Sprinkle the garnish over the lamb and serve.

Serves 4

*Note: The lamb is cooked very slowly in this Italian recipe, leaving it meltingly tender. There should be enough to satisfy the biggest appetites. Serve with pasta ribbons or mashed potato.*

# Mushrooms Stuffed with Pork and Sage

(see photograph opposite)

8 very large open mushrooms
   or 16 open cup mushrooms

1 tablespoon vegetable oil

1 onion, finely chopped

2 cloves garlic, finely chopped

375g fresh minced pork

2 cups fresh breadcrumbs

1 tablespoon chopped fresh sage or
   parsley, plus extra leaves to garnish

1 medium egg, beaten

salt and black pepper

1   Preheat the oven to 190°C. Remove any stalks from the mushrooms and finely chop them. Heat the oil in a large heavy-based frying pan and fry the chopped stalks, onion, and garlic for 3–5 minutes, until softened. Add the pork and cook for 5 minutes, stirring, until it browns.

2   Transfer the mixture to a bowl. Stir in the breadcrumbs, sage or parsley, and enough beaten egg to lightly bind the mixture. Season well.

3   Divide the stuffing between the mushrooms, using a spoon. Place on a baking sheet and bake for 20 minutes or until mushrooms have softened and the topping is golden. Scatter with the sage or parsley leaves.

Serves 4

*Note: Large mushrooms are crammed with a delicious mixture of herby pork and golden breadcrumbs. Serve with a salad and some lightly buttered new potatoes.*

# Meatballs with Tomato Relish

250g brown onions, finely chopped

1 kg minced beef

½ cup breadcrumbs

2 eggs

1 tablespoon mint, chopped

¼ cup water

salt and freshly ground black pepper

2 cups vegetable oil, for frying

sprinkle of plain flour

**TOMATO RELISH**

1 kg plum tomatoes, chopped

2 brown onions, chopped

1 cup sugar

½ cup brown vinegar

2 tablespoons tomato pureé

1 teaspoon salt

½ tablespoon dry mustard

¼ teaspoon cayenne pepper (optional)

**MEATBALLS**

1  In a bowl, combine the chopped onions, minced beef, breadcrumbs, eggs, mint, water, and salt and pepper. Squeeze the mixture between your fingers making sure it's well combined.

2  Using 2 tablespoons of mixture for each meatball, shape into balls, then toss in a little flour, and shake off the excess. Flatten each ball slightly into the palm of your hand.

3  Heat the oil in a pan and cook each meatball for approximately 3 minutes each side until they are  dark brown and cooked through.

4  Drain on absorbent paper.

**TOMATO RELISH**

1  Place all ingredients in a medium-sized saucepan and bring to a boil, then simmer for one hour (until mixture becomes thick and pulpy). Check the seasoning, and add salt and black pepper if desired.

2  Remove from the heat and store in a sterilised jar in the refrigerator for up to one week. With the remainder of the Tomato Relish, serve hot or cold with the meatballs.

Makes 40

# Yorkshire Pudding with Minced Beef

½ cup plain flour

salt and black pepper

2 medium eggs

1¼ cups milk

2 tablespoons vegetable oil

1 onion, chopped

1 carrot, chopped

1 cup mushrooms, chopped

375g minced beef

1 cup canned chopped tomatoes

1 cup baked beans

fresh parsley to garnish

1  Sift the flour and a pinch of salt into a bowl, then make a well in the centre. Break the eggs into the well. Beat the eggs, gradually drawing in the flour and adding the milk a little at a time until it forms a smooth batter. Cover and leave for 30 minutes.

2  Preheat the oven to 220°C. Heat 1 tablespoon of oil in a large, heavy-based frying pan and cook the onion and carrot for 5 minutes or until softened. Add the mushrooms and cook for 2–3 minutes, then stir in the minced beef and cook for 5 minutes or until browned. Add the tomatoes and cook for 15 minutes. Stir in the beans, heat for 5 minutes, season and keep warm.

3  Meanwhile, divide the remaining oil between 4 Yorkshire pudding tins. Place in the oven for 5 minutes or until the oil is hot. Pour in the batter and cook for 20–25 minutes, until risen and crisp. Place on serving plates, spoon in the minced beef and garnish with the parsley.

**Serves 4**

*Note: These Yorkshire pudding cases are delicious with a variety of fillings. Try them with chicken curry, meatballs in tomato sauce or a thick vegetable ratatouille.*

# Lamb and Pepper Kebabs with Chilli Sauce

½ cup red wine

1 tablespoon olive oil

juice of ½ lemon

1 tablespoon chopped fresh rosemary

freshly ground black pepper

375g lean boneless leg of lamb, cut into 12 cubes

1 red and 1 yellow pepper, each deseeded and cut into 8 pieces

16 button mushrooms

4 metal skewers

## SAUCE

2 cups canned chopped tomatoes

½ cup vegetable stock

1 small onion, finely chopped

1 green chilli, deseeded and finely chopped

1 tablespoon tomato pureé

1 clove garlic, crushed

freshly ground black pepper

## KEBABS

1  In a non-metallic bowl, mix 4 tablespoons of the red wine and the oil, lemon juice, rosemary and black pepper. Add the lamb, turn to coat, then cover and place in the fridge for 2 hours.

2  Preheat the grill to high. Thread the lamb, peppers and mushrooms onto 4 metal skewers, dividing evenly. Reserve the marinade.

3  Meanwhile, grill the kebabs for 12–18 minutes until the lamb is tender, turning occasionally and basting with the marinade. Serve with the chilli sauce.

## SAUCE

1  Place the tomatoes, stock, onion, chilli, tomato pureé, garlic, black pepper and remaining wine in a saucepan and stir. Bring to a boil, then reduce the heat and simmer, uncovered, for 15–20 minutes, until the sauce has thickened, stirring occasionally.

### Serves 4

*Note: The rosemary in the marinade goes beautifully with large succulent chunks of lamb, while a hot chilli sauce adds some bite. If you prefer, use apple juice instead of wine.*

# Lamb and Apricot Casserole

1 tablespoon sunflower oil

500g lean boneless lamb leg or fillet,
  cut into 25mm cubes

1 large onion, chopped

1 clove garlic, finely chopped

2 tablespoons plain flour

1 teaspoon ground coriander

1 teaspoon ground cumin

1½ cups vegetable stock

⅔ cup red wine

1 cup baby button mushrooms

1 tablespoon tomato pureé

1 bouquet garni

freshly ground black pepper

1 cup dried apricots

2 tablespoons chopped fresh coriander,
  plus extra leaves to garnish

1  Preheat the oven to 160°C. Heat the oil in a flameproof and ovenproof casserole dish on the stove. Add the lamb and cook for about 5 minutes or until browned. Remove and keep warm.

2  Add the onion and garlic to the juices in the dish and cook for 5 minutes, or until softened. Return the lamb to the dish with the flour, coriander, and cumin, and cook for 1 minute, stirring. Slowly add the stock and wine and bring to the boil, stirring. Stir in the mushrooms, tomato pureé, bouquet garni, and pepper. Cover and cook in the oven for 1 hour.

3  Stir in the apricots and cook for a further 30 minutes or until the lamb is tender. Remove and discard the bouquet garni, stir in the chopped coriander, then garnish with more fresh coriander.

**Serves 4**

*Note: Dried apricots give a sweetness to this delicious casserole, but dried pears or peaches also work well. Serve it with some steamed broccoli and bread, rice or jacket potatoes.*

# Peppered Beef Steaks with Red Onion Salsa

2 tablespoons mixed peppercorns

4 lean sirloin, rump or fillet steaks, trimmed of fat

fresh parsley to garnish

### SALSA

3 tomatoes

2 tablespoons tomato juice

2 tablespoons olive oil

1 red onion, finely chopped

2 teaspoons horseradish sauce

1 tablespoon chopped fresh parsley

freshly ground black pepper

### SALSA

1  Place the tomatoes in a bowl, cover with boiling water and leave for 30 seconds. Drain, peel off the skins, deseed and finely chop. Put the flesh into a bowl with the tomato juice, ½ the oil, the red onion, horseradish sauce, parsley and black pepper, and mix together well. Cover and set aside for 1 hour.

### STEAK

1  Preheat the grill to medium. Crush the peppercorns with a pestle and mortar, or rolling pin. Brush the steaks all over with the rest of the oil, then coat with the crushed peppercorns.

2  Place the steaks on the grill rack and grill for 4–5 minutes each side, until browned and cooked to your liking. Serve with the red onion salsa and garnish with the fresh parsley.

Serves 4

# Spiced Beef and Carrot Burgers

500g extra lean minced beef

2 carrots, coarsely grated

1 cup mushrooms, finely chopped

1 large onion or 3 spring onions,
   finely chopped

1 cup fresh whole-wheat breadcrumbs

2 tablespoons tomato purée

1 medium egg, lightly beaten

1 clove garlic, crushed

2 teaspoons ground cumin

2 teaspoons ground coriander

1 teaspoon hot chilli powder

freshly ground black pepper

1 Preheat the grill to medium. Place all the ingredients in a large bowl and mix
   together well.

2 Shape the mixture into 4 round, flat burgers, using your hands. Grill for about
   10–15 minutes, until the burgers are lightly browned and cooked to your
   liking, turning once.

**Serves 4**

*Note: These healthy burgers will be popular with all the family. Try serving
them in wholemeal buns piled high with crisp salad leaves, slices of tomato,
and tangy relish.*

# Spiced Lamb and Apricot Pilau

1 tablespoon vegetable oil

1 onion, chopped

2 cloves garlic, chopped

500g neck of lamb or stewing lamb off
the bone, cut into 25mm cubes

1 teaspoon turmeric

1 teaspoon ground cumin

½ teaspoon ground cinnamon

1 tablespoon grated fresh root ginger

1¼ cups long-grain white rice

2 cups canned chopped tomatoes

1¼ cups vegetable or lamb stock

¾ cup ready-to-eat dried apricots,
chopped

⅓ cup seedless raisins

salt and black pepper

3 tablespoons toasted flaked almonds
(optional)

1 Heat the oil in a large heavy-based saucepan and cook the onion, garlic and lamb for 5 minutes, or until the onion and garlic have softened and the meat has browned. Stir in the turmeric, cumin, cinnamon and ginger, then cook for 1 minute, stirring, to release their flavours.

2 Add the rice and cook, stirring, for 1 minute to coat well. Add the tomatoes and ½ the stock, then stir in the apricots and raisins. Cover and cook gently for 10 minutes.  Check the mixture from time to time and add a little more stock if it starts to dry out. Add ½ of the remaining stock and cook for a further 10 minutes. Then add the rest of the stock and cook for 30–35 minutes, stirring, until the rice is tender and all the liquid is absorbed. Add a little extra water if the mixture becomes too dry.

3 Season to taste and remove from the heat. Cover and leave to stand for 5 minutes. Serve sprinkled with the almonds (if using).

**Serves 4**

Note: In this dish, apricots, long-grain rice and tender chunks of lamb are simmered in a spicy stock. It's all cooked in one pot, so there's hardly any washing up.

# Carbonada Griolla

2 tablespoons oil

1 clove garlic, crushed

1 large onion, chopped

1 kg boned shoulder of veal, cut into 25mm cubes

1 cup peeled, canned tomatoes

1½ cups beef stock

1 teaspoon chopped thyme

2 tablespoons chopped parsley

salt and pepper

1 medium potato, cubed

1 sweet potato, cubed

250g pumpkin, cubed

2 fresh corn cobs, cut into thick slices

½ cup short grain rice

4 large dried peaches, halved

4 large dried pears, halved

1 Heat the oil in a large saucepan and sauté the garlic and onion. Add the veal, and quickly stir over a high heat to brown lightly.

2 Add the tomatoes, stock, thyme and parsley and season with salt and pepper. Bring to the boil, then turn down the heat and simmer for 25 minutes.

3 Add the cubed vegetables, corn, rice and dried fruits. Cover and simmer for 25 minutes. Stir occasionally during cooking and add extra stock if necessary. Adjust seasoning before serving.

Serves 6

# Ham Steaks with Fruity Sauce

## FRUITY SAUCE

½ cup mixed dried fruit

1½ cups water

½ teaspoon salt

2 tablespoons brown sugar

1 teaspoon Worcestershire sauce

3–4 drops Tabasco sauce

1 tablespoon cornflour blended with a
  little water

## HAM STEAKS

butter for frying

6 ham steaks

## HAM STEAKS

1   Heat the butter in a frying pan and fry the ham steaks on both sides until rosy brown. Serve the with fruity sauce and vegetable accompaniments.

## FRUITY SAUCE

1   To make the fruity sauce, place the mixed dried fruit in a saucepan, add the water and soak for ½ hour. Add the remaining sauce ingredients (except the cornflour) and bring to a boil. Turn down and simmer, covered, for 20 minutes. Add the blended cornflour and stir until the sauce thickens.

Serves 3–4

# Mushroom and Tarragon Stuffed Chicken

2 tablespoons olive oil

1 small leek, finely chopped

1 small courgette, finely chopped

1 clove garlic, crushed

½ cup button mushrooms, finely
chopped

½ cup oyster or shiitake mushrooms,
finely chopped

1 tablespoon chopped fresh tarragon,
plus extra leaves to garnish

freshly ground black pepper

4 skinless boneless chicken breasts

cocktail sticks

1  Preheat the oven to 180°C. Heat half the oil in a saucepan. Add the leek, courgette, garlic and mushrooms, and cook for 5 minutes, stirring, until softened. Remove from the heat and stir in the tarragon and  pepper.

2  Place the chicken breasts between 2 large sheets of baking paper. Beat to an even thickness with a rolling pin. Spread the stuffing evenly over each breast. Roll up, folding in the ends and secure with wetted cocktail sticks. Brush with the remaining oil and place on a non-stick baking sheet.

3  Cook in the oven for 30–35 minutes, until the juices run clear when pierced with a skewer. Remove the cocktail sticks and cut each roll into 2cm slices, then garnish with fresh tarragon.

Serves 4

*Note: The aniseed flavour of fresh tarragon combines beautifully with chicken and mushrooms. Try serving these neat slices with potatoes and some roasted cherry tomatoes.*

# Turkey Steaks with Mustard Sauce

1 tablespoon olive oil

4 skinless boneless turkey breast steaks

**SAUCE**

1 tablespoon sunflower spread

1 tablespoon plain flour

1 cups low-fat milk

1–2 tablespoons wholegrain mustard

freshly ground black pepper

fresh herbs, such as basil, chives or
  coriander to garnish

1 Heat the oil in a non-stick frying pan. Add the turkey steaks and cook for
15 minutes, or until tender and lightly browned, turning once.

2 Meanwhile, melt the sunflower spread in a saucepan. Add the flour and
gently cook for 1 minute, stirring. Remove from the heat and gradually add
the milk, stirring until smooth.

3 Return to the heat and slowly bring to the boil, stirring continuously until the
sauce thickens. Simmer for 2 minutes, stirring occasionally. Stir in the mustard
and pepper.

4 Spoon the mustard sauce over the turkey steaks and serve garnished with the
fresh herbs.

Serves 4

# Lamb with Roast Pepper Purée

1 clove garlic, crushed

¼ cup white wine

2 tablespoons tarragon vinegar

2 tablespoons wholegrain mustard

1 tablespoon honey

8 lamb cutlets, trimmed of
all visible fat

## ROAST PEPPER PURÉE

1 red pepper, seeded and quartered

1 yellow pepper, seeded and quartered

100g low-fat yoghurt

2 tablespoons chopped fresh mint

### PURÉE

1  Place red and yellow peppers, skin side up, under a preheated hot grill and cook for 10–15 minutes or until skins are blistered and charred. Place peppers in a plastic food bag or paper bag and set aside until cool enough to handle, then remove skins. Place peppers and yoghurt in a food processor or blender and process to make a purée. Stir in mint and set aside.

### LAMB

1  Place garlic, wine, vinegar, mustard and honey in a shallow glass or ceramic dish and mix to combine. Add lamb, cover and marinate in the refrigerator for 3–4 hours or overnight.

2  Drain lamb and cook under a preheated medium grill or on a barbecue for 3–5 minutes each side or until lamb is cooked to your liking. Serve with the purée.

Serves 4

# Duck Breasts with Chilli

4 boneless duck breasts, about 150g each

**DRESSING**

juice of 2 large oranges, plus few strips of zest to garnish

1 green chilli, deseeded and finely chopped

½ cup dry vermouth or sherry

1 tablespoon redcurrant jelly

salt and black pepper

**DRESSING**

1 Place the orange juice, chilli, vermouth or sherry, redcurrant jelly and seasoning in the pan. Boil vigorously, stirring constantly, for 5 minutes or until reduced and glossy.

**DUCK**

1 Preheat the oven to 220°C. Score the skin of each duck breast in a diamond pattern. Heat a heavy based frying pan until hot and place the breasts, skin-side down, in the pan. Cook over a medium to high heat for 5 minutes or until the skin is browned and crispy.

2 Pour off the hot fat, turn over the duck and cook for 5 minutes. Place the duck, skin-side up, on the rack of a roasting tin and roast in the oven for 10 minutes. Rest in a warm place for 5 minutes.

3 Slice the duck very thinly. Serve with the dressing poured over and garnished with the orange zest.

Serves 4

*Note: Quickly pan-frying the duck, then roasting it, is a technique that many chefs use to make the meat really succulent. Serve on a bed of bitter salad leaves or rocket.*

# Beef with Artichokes, Olives and Oregano

2 tablespoons olive oil

750g scotch fillet

1 clove garlic, crushed

1 bunch spring onions, trimmed and halved

½ cup white wine

1 cup beef stock

1 tablespoon tomato pureé

2 teaspoons oregano, chopped

salt and freshly ground pepper

2 globe artichokes, trimmed and quartered

⅓ cup olives, pitted

1 Preheat the oven to 180°C.

2 In a large, heavy-based oven-proof dish, heat 1 tablespoon olive oil, add the meat and sear quickly on all sides. Remove and set aside.

3 Heat remaining olive oil, add the garlic and spring onions, and cook for 2–3 minutes. Add the white wine, cook for 1 minute, then add the beef stock, tomato pureé, oregano and salt and pepper. Bring to the boil, return the meat to the dish, add the artichokes, cover and bake for 30–40 minutes.

4 Add the olives in the last 5 minutes of cooking time.

5 Slice the meat and arrange with the vegetables. Pour the sauce over meat and vegetables.

**Serves 4**

Note: Trim the artichokes of their outer leaves and stems and place them in a bowl of water with lemon juice to stop them going brown.

# Lamb Shanks with Broad Beans, Olives and Risoni

2 tablespoons olive oil

2 cloves garlic, crushed

4 lamb shanks

1 onion, chopped

2 cups beef stock

4 sprigs oregano

2 tablespoons tomato pureé

2 cups water

1 cup risoni (rice)

1 cup broad beans

½ cup olives

2 teaspoons fresh oregano, chopped

salt and freshly ground pepper

1  Heat the oil in a large saucepan, add the garlic, lamb shanks and onion and cook for 5 minutes or until the shanks are lightly browned.

2  Add the beef stock, oregano sprigs, tomato pureé and ½ the water. Bring to the boil, reduce the heat and leave to simmer with the lid on for 40 minutes.

3  Remove the shanks, slice the meat off the bone and set aside.

4  Add the risoni and the remaining water, cook for a further 5 minutes, then add the beans, olives, meat, oregano, salt and pepper, cook for 5 minutes more and serve.

Serves 4–6

*Note: If broad beans are large, peel off outer skin.*

# fish and shellfish

# Poached Salmon with Asparagus

(see photograph on page 56)

4 skinless salmon fillets

freshly ground black pepper

¾ cup vegetable stock

¾ cup dry white wine

2 bay leaves

20 asparagus spears

1 tablespoon olive oil

snipped fresh chives to garnish

1 lemon, cut into wedges to serve

1 Place the salmon in a large, shallow frying pan and season with pepper. Mix together the stock and wine and pour over the fish. Add the bay leaves and cover the pan.

2 Bring to the boil, then reduce the heat and simmer very gently for 10 minutes, or until the fish is cooked and the flesh is just beginning to flake.

3 Meanwhile, preheat the grill to high. Lightly brush the asparagus with the oil and place on the grill rack. Grill for 5–7 minutes, until the asparagus is tender and lightly browned, turning occasionally.

4 Using a fish slice, remove the fish from the stock and place on serving plates with the asparagus. Garnish with a sprinkling of fresh chives and serve with the lemon wedges.

### Serves 4

*Note: Poaching salmon is really easy and it stops the fish from becoming too dry. You can freeze the leftover stock for up to 2 months and use it for making soups or sauces.*

# Chargrilled Tuna with Peach Salsa

(see photograph opposite)

4 tuna steaks

1 tablespoon olive oil

black pepper

chopped fresh coriander to garnish

1 lime cut into wedges to serve

**SALSA**

3 ripe peaches, peeled, stoned, and finely chopped

4 spring onions, finely chopped

½ cup yellow pepper, deseeded and finely chopped

juice of ½ lime

1 tablespoon chopped fresh coriander

black pepper

**SALSA**

1 Place the peaches, spring onions, pepper, lime juice, coriander and black pepper in a small bowl and mix well. Cover and set aside for at least 1 hour to let the flavours mingle.

**TUNA**

1 Preheat the grill to high. Brush the tuna with the oil and season with black pepper. Grill for 3–5 minutes each side, until the fish is cooked and the flesh is beginning to flake. Garnish with the fresh coriander and serve with the lime wedges and peach salsa.

### Serves 4

*Note: Fresh tuna steaks are a treat on their own, but served with this peach salsa they're absolutely fabulous! The salsa also goes well with ham and pork.*

# Marinated Fish Kebabs

4 wooden skewers

1 kg skinless boneless white fish fillet, cut into 25mm cubes

4 button onions or small spring onions, halved

1 small red and 1 small yellow pepper, each deseeded and cut into 8 – 12 chunks

1 small courgette, cut into 12 thin slices

finely grated zest and juice of 1 lemon

2 tablespoons freshly squeezed orange juice

1 tablespoon dry sherry

2 teaspoons clear honey

2 cloves garlic, crushed

freshly ground black pepper

fresh herbs, such as rosemary, marjoram and basil, to garnish

1 Soak the skewers in water for 10 minutes while preparing the vegetables. Thread equal amounts of the fish, onions or spring onions, peppers, and courgettes onto each skewer.

2 Place the kebabs in a shallow non-metallic dish in a single layer. In a small bowl, mix together the lemon zest and juice and the orange juice, sherry, honey, garlic and black pepper, and pour over the kebabs. Turn to coat all over, then cover and refrigerate for 2 hours.

3 Preheat the grill to medium. Grill the kebabs for 10–15 minutes, until the fish is tender, turning occasionally. Baste frequently with the marinade to keep the kebabs moist. Garnish with the fresh herbs.

**Serves 4**

# Seafood and Broccoli Risotto

1 tablespoon sunflower oil

6 spring onions, chopped

1 clove garlic, finely chopped

1 red or yellow pepper, deseeded and diced

1 cup arborio rice

2 cups vegetable stock

1½ cups chestnut mushrooms, sliced

1 cup dry white wine

500g frozen seafood selection, defrosted

250g broccoli, cut into small florets

2 tablespoons chopped fresh flat-leaf parsley

freshly ground black pepper

1 Heat the oil in a large saucepan, add the spring onions, garlic and pepper and cook for 5 minutes or until softened, stirring occasionally. Add the rice and cook for 1 minute, stirring, until well coated in the oil.

2 In a separate pan, bring the stock to the boil. Add the mushrooms, wine and ¼ cup of the stock to the rice mixture. Bring to a boil, stirring, then simmer, uncovered, for 15 minutes or until most of the liquid is absorbed, stirring often. Add another cup of stock and cook for 15 minutes or until it's absorbed, stirring frequently.

3 Add the seafood and most of the remaining stock and stir frequently for 5 minutes or until the rice is cooked but firm to the bite. Add the rest of the stock, if necessary, and make sure the seafood is cooked through. Meanwhile, cook the broccoli in boiling water for 3 minutes or until tender. Drain well, stir into the risotto with the parsley and season with black pepper.

**Serves 4**

*Note: The secret to cooking a good risotto is to keep adding just enough liquid and to stir as much as possible. You can use any mixture of seafood – prawns and mussels are good.*

# Mussels Marinieres

1 kg mussels, cleaned

1 small onion, sliced

1 stick of celery, sliced

1 garlic clove, chopped

6 tablespoon water or white wine

pepper

1 tablespoon butter

1 tablespoon parsley, chopped

1 Place mussels, onion, celery, garlic and water or white wine in a large saucepan.

2 Cook over a medium heat until the mussels have opened. Stir frequently to ensure the mussels cook evenly.

3 Add pepper to taste. Stir in the butter and parsley just before serving.

Serves 3–4

# Baked Cod with Ginger and Spring Onions

1 tablespoon vegetable oil for greasing

500g piece cod fillet

1 tablespoon light soy sauce

1 tablespoon rice wine or medium-dry sherry

1 teaspoon sesame oil

salt

3 spring onions, shredded and cut into 25mm pieces, white and green parts separated

25mm piece fresh root ginger, finely chopped

1 Preheat the oven to 190°C. Line a shallow baking dish with a piece of lightly greased foil.

2 Place the cod in the dish, skin-side down. Pour over the soy sauce, rice wine or sherry, oil and salt to taste, then sprinkle over the white parts of the spring onions and the ginger.

3 Loosely wrap the foil over the fish, folding the edges together to seal. Bake for 20–25 minutes, until cooked through and tender. Unwrap the parcel, transfer the fish to a serving plate and sprinkle over the green parts of the spring onions to garnish.

**Serves 4**

*Note: One of the best ways to prepare fish is to bake it in a foil parcel so that it cooks in its own juices. Here, sesame oil, ginger and spring onions add a Chinese twist.*

# Greek Tuna Focaccia

2 x 10cm squares focaccia bread

90g marinated or plain feta cheese, crumbled

½ bunch rocket or watercress, broken into sprigs

440g canned tuna in brine or springwater, drained

60g sun-dried tomatoes in oil, drained and sliced

1 tablespoon capers, drained

1 onion, thinly sliced into rings

1 tablespoon chopped fresh dill

1 Split focaccia bread horizontally and toast lightly under a preheated medium grill.

2 Top each piece of bread with feta cheese, rocket or watercress, tuna, sun-dried tomatoes, capers and onion rings. Sprinkle with dill.

Serves 4

# Salmon with Asparagus, Balsamic Vinegar and Orange

2 tablespoon extra virgin olive oil

finely grated zest of ½ orange, plus juice of 1 orange

sea salt and freshly ground black pepper

250g asparagus, trimmed

4 salmon steaks, about 170g each

1 tablespoon balsamic vinegar

2 tablespoons chopped fresh coriander

1 Preheat the oven to 200°C. Place 1 tablespoon of the oil on a baking tray with the orange zest and seasoning. Add asparagus and toss well in the oil mixture. Cook for 15–20 minutes or until tender.

2 Meanwhile, wash and wipe the salmon with kitchen paper and season. Heat the remaining oil in a large frying pan over a medium heat. Add the salmon to the pan and cook for 4–5 minutes each side, or until golden and cooked through.

3 Add the vinegar and orange juice and simmer for about 2 minutes, until the sauce is bubbling and warmed through. Stir in the coriander and serve immediately with the asparagus.

**Serves 4**

*Note: The tangy citrus flavours and balsamic vinegar cut through the richness of the salmon. It's delicious served simply with new potatoes. The zest of organic citrus fruit can be used in cooking without worrying about the wax, which non-organic fruit is sometimes sprayed with to make it shiny. Oranges are an excellent source of Vitamin C.*

# Steamed Ginger Chilli Mussels

1 kg mussels, scrubbed and beards removed

## GINGER CHILLI SAUCE

5cm piece fresh ginger, finely chopped

3 cloves garlic, crushed

1 stalk lemongrass, finely chopped or 1 teaspoon dried lemongrass soaked in hot water until soft

3 small fresh red chillies, finely sliced

3 spring onions, diagonally sliced

4 tablespoons, coriander leaves

60ml white wine

2 tablespoons, rice vinegar

1 tablespoon Thai fish sauce (nam pla)

2 teaspoons sesame oil

## GINGER CHILLI SAUCE

1   Place ginger, garlic, lemongrass, chillies, spring onions, coriander, wine, vinegar, fish sauce and sesame oil in a bowl and mix to combine. Set aside.

## MUSSELS

1   Place mussels in a large steamer, set over a saucepan of boiling water, cover and steam for 5 minutes or until mussels open. Discard any mussels that do not open after 5 minutes cooking. Spoon sauce over mussels and heat for 1 minute longer. Serve immediately.

Serves 4

*Note: It may be necessary to steam the mussels in batches. For a complete meal, serve with boiled brown or white rice and steamed vegetables of your choice.*

# Spicy Seafood Stir-Fry

2 squid tubes

1 tablespoon sesame oil

1 onion, cut into wedges and layers
separated

2 teaspoons finely chopped fresh ginger

1 clove garlic, crushed

2 teaspoons chilli paste (sambal oelek)

1 red pepper, chopped

1 yellow pepper, chopped

2 tablespoons lime juice

1 tablespoon honey

375g medium raw prawns, shelled and
deveined

90g scallops, cleaned

125g green beans, cut into 2½ cm
pieces

125g mangetout

¼ cup coconut milk

**1** Make a single cut down the length of each squid tube and open out. Using a sharp knife, cut parallel lines down the length of the squid, taking care not to cut right through the flesh. Make more cuts in the opposite direction to form a diamond pattern. Cut each piece into 2½ cm squares. Set aside.

**2** Heat oil in a wok or frying pan over a high heat, add onion, ginger, garlic and chilli paste (sambal oelek) and stir-fry for 2 minutes or until onion is golden. Add red pepper, yellow pepper, lime juice and honey and stir-fry for 2 minutes longer.

**3** Add squid, prawns and scallops and stir-fry for 5 minutes or until prawns just change colour. Add beans, mangetout and coconut milk and cook for 2 minutes or until seafood is cooked.

Serves 4

# Tuna Bean Salad

375g dried haricot beans

1 onion, halved

440g canned tuna, drained and flaked

4 spring onions, chopped

1 red pepper, diced

4 tablespoons chopped fresh parsley

4 tablespoons olive oil

2 tablespoons cider vinegar

freshly ground black pepper

1 Place beans in a large bowl, cover with water and set aside to soak overnight, then drain. Place beans and onion in a saucepan with enough water to cover and bring to the boil. Boil for 10 minutes, then reduce heat and simmer for 1 hour or until beans are tender. Remove onion and discard, drain beans and set aside to cool.

2 Place beans, tuna, spring onions, red pepper and parsley in a salad bowl.

3 Place oil, vinegar and black pepper to taste in a screwtop jar and shake well to combine. Pour dressing over bean mixture and toss to combine. Serve immediately.

**Serves 6**

# Sardines Stuffed with Spinach and Pine Nuts

8 fresh sardines

salt and black pepper

2 tablespoons olive oil

1 spring onion, finely chopped

1 tablespoon pine nut kernels

2 cups frozen leaf spinach, defrosted and excess moisture squeezed out

1 tablespoon sultanas

2 tablespoons fresh breadcrumbs

1 tablespoon lime juice

1 Preheat the oven to 220°C. Remove the scales from the fish by scraping them from the tail end with the back of a small knife. Cut off the heads, then slice along belly and remove the innards. Open out each fish and place skin-side up on the work surface. Press along the length of the backbone with your thumb, then turn the fish over and ease out the backbone, cutting it at the tail end but leaving the tail intact. Rinse and pat dry with kitchen towels, season and turn in 1 tablespoon of the oil.

2 Heat the remaining oil in a frying pan and fry the spring onion and pine nut kernels for 2–3 minutes, until golden. Remove from the heat, then stir in the spinach, sultanas, 1 tablespoon of the breadcrumbs, and the lime juice. Season, then use the mixture to sandwich the sardines together in pairs, skin-side out.

3 Lay the sardines on a baking sheet, sprinkle with the remaining breadcrumbs, and bake for 10 minutes or until golden and cooked through.

**Serves 4**

# Lemon-Scented Fish Pie

1 kg potatoes, cut into even-sized pieces

salt and black pepper

4 tablespoons butter

1 onion, chopped

2 sticks celery, sliced

2 tablespoons plain flour

1 cup fish stock

finely grated zest and juice of 1 large lemon

500g cod loin, cubed

250g cooked and shelled mussels

2 tablespoons chopped fresh parsley

4 tablespoons milk

1 Cook the potatoes in boiling salted water for 15–20 minutes, until tender, then drain.

2 Meanwhile, melt ⅓ of the butter in a large saucepan, then add the onion and celery and cook for 2–3 minutes, until softened. Add the flour and cook, stirring, for 1 minute, then slowly add the stock and cook, stirring, until thickened. Add the lemon zest and juice and season with pepper.

3 Preheat the oven to 220°C. Remove the sauce from heat, stir in the cod, mussels and parsley then transfer to an ovenproof dish. Mash the potatoes with the remaining butter and the milk. Season, then spread evenly over the fish with a fork. Cook in the oven for 30–40 minutes, until the sauce is bubbling and the topping starts to brown.

**Serves 4**

*Note: Creamy mashed potatoes make a wonderful topping for this lemon-flavoured cod and mussel pie. If you wish, replace the mussels with peeled prawns.*

# Seared Tuna with Roasted Plum Tomato

1 clove garlic, finely chopped

finely grated zest and juice of 1 lime

5 tablespoons olive oil, plus extra for greasing

3 tablespoons chopped rosemary

4 tuna steaks, about 145g each and 25mm thick

6 plum tomatoes, halved lengthways

1 red onion, halved and thinly sliced lengthways

salt and black pepper

1 Mix together the garlic, lime zest, ½ the lime juice, 2 tablespoons of the oil, and 1 tablespoon of the rosemary in a large dish. Add the tuna and turn to coat evenly. Cover and place in the fridge for 30 minutes to marinate.

2 Preheat the oven to 220°C. Place the tomatoes and onion in a shallow ovenproof dish with the remaining rosemary. Drizzle with the remaining oil and season. Roast in the oven for 15–20 minutes, until tender and lightly browned.

3 Lightly oil a ridged cast-iron grill pan or large frying pan and heat over a fairly high heat. Add the tuna and cook, turning once for 4–5 minutes or until golden. Serve with the tomatoes and onion, sprinkled with the remaining lime juice.

**Serves 4**

*Note: Lightly pan-fried tuna is delicious with just a squeeze of lemon or lime juice. But it's the roasted tomatoes, scented with rosemary, that make this dish hard to beat.*

# Salmon Parcels with Asparagus, Ginger and Lime

4 thick pieces salmon fillet, about 5cm wide

2 limes

4 x 40cm-long pieces baking paper

1 tablespoon grated root ginger

16 spears fresh or frozen asparagus

1  Remove skin from salmon if wished. Remove fine pin bones using a pair of clean tweezers. Cut eight thin slices from one lime.

2  Place a piece of fish in the middle of each piece of paper. Sprinkle ginger over fish. Squeeze juice from remaining lime over and lay two slices of lime on top of each fish piece. Break woody ends from asparagus and place asparagus on fish. Wrap paper around salmon to form a tight parcel. Tie with string if wished as a novel way to present this.

3  Place in an ovenproof dish and bake at 180°C for 15 minutes. Serve tied parcels or cut paper open and serve salmon in paper.

**Serves 4**

*Note: Substitute lemons for limes if preferred in this recipe. If asparagus is unavailable, use other vegetables such as bok choy, spinach or sliced courgette.*

*Wrapping food in paper to cook it captures all the flavour. The food cooks by steaming and the paper-wrapped parcel can be cooked in water or baked in the oven. If preferred, cook these salmon parcels immersed in a frying pan or electric frying pan half-filled with water. Cooking time will be slightly shorter.*

# vegetable dishes

# Bubble and Squeak with Red Onion Chutney

(see photograph on page 78)

750g potatoes, peeled and cut into even-sized pieces

1 garlic clove, peeled

1 cup cabbage, finely shredded

4 spring onions, finely sliced

sea salt and freshly ground black pepper

2 tablespoons butter

1 tablespoon sunflower oil

**RED ONION CHUTNEY**

2 large red onions, or 6 small red onions, finely chopped

4 tablespoons brown sugar

1 tablespoon white wine vinegar

1  Place the potatoes and garlic in a saucepan and cover with water. Bring to the boil, cover and simmer for 15–20 minutes, until tender. Drain, return to the pan and mash until smooth. Cool.

2  Meanwhile, place the cabbage in a saucepan and pour over boiling water to just cover, bring back to the boil, then drain. Add the cabbage, spring onions, and seasoning to the potato and mix well.

3  Divide the potato into 8 and shape into flat rounds. Melt the butter and oil in a frying pan and fry the cakes for 5 minutes on 1 side over a medium heat. Turn over, taking care as the cakes are quite soft, and cook for a further 5 minutes, until golden and heated through. Serve with the chutney.

**RED ONION CHUTNEY**

1  Place all the ingredients for the chutney in a saucepan and bring to the boil over a low heat. Simmer gently, uncovered, for about 20 minutes or until almost all the liquid has evaporated.

**Serves 4**

*Note: Originally a recipe to use up leftovers from the Sunday roast, bubble and squeak is now found on the smartest restaurant menus. It's wonderful with the sweet chutney.*

# Vegetable Tempura

(see photograph opposite)

2 eggs

½ cup ice-cold water

½ cup plain flour, sieved

1 cup cranberry and orange sauce, for dipping

2 cups vegetable oil, for deep-frying

1 courgette, cut into thick slices

1 large red onion, cut into wedges

250g broccoli, cut into small florets

1 red pepper, deseeded and cut into strips

1 cup green beans, topped only (not tailed)

1 cup asparagus, trimmed

sea salt

fresh basil leaves to garnish (optional)

1  To make the batter, lightly whisk together the eggs and water, then pour onto the flour all at once and whisk quickly, until the batter is smooth.

2  Heat the cranberry and orange sauce in a small saucepan, over a gentle heat, until warm and runny. Remove from the heat and place in a bowl.

3  Heat 5cm of oil in a wok or frying pan. Dip the vegetables in the batter and coat well. Test the temperature of the oil by dropping in a little batter; if it floats straight back to the surface the oil is hot enough.

4  Deep-fry the vegetables in small batches for 3–4 minutes or until crisp and golden. Remove with a slotted spoon and drain on kitchen paper. Season with salt. If using, deep-fry a few basil leaves for 20 seconds, until crisp. Serve immediately with the dipping sauce.

**Serves 4**

# Stuffed Tomatoes with Chickpeas and Coriander

2 slices day-old brown bread

4 large slicing tomatoes

1 clove garlic, crushed

½ cup canned chickpeas, drained

juice of 1 lemon

1 tablespoon olive oil, plus extra for greasing

1 red onion, finely chopped

¼ teaspoon cayenne pepper

1 teaspoon ground cumin

1 teaspoon ground coriander

4 tablespoons chopped fresh coriander

salt and black pepper

1 Preheat the oven to 160°C. Place the bread in oven for 20 minutes or until it becomes crisp. Process in a food processor to make breadcrumbs. Alternatively, use a grater. Increase the oven temperature to 200°C.

2 Slice off the tomato tops and scoop out the insides. Place the shells upside down on kitchen towels to drain. Put the insides and tops into a food processor with the garlic, chickpeas and lemon juice and blend to a purée, or use a hand blender.

3 Heat the oil, then cook the onion with the cayenne pepper, cumin and ground coriander for 4–5 minutes, until softened. Mix with the tomato mixture, breadcrumbs, fresh coriander and seasoning.

4 Spoon the mixture into the tomato shells. Place them on a lightly greased baking sheet and cook for 25 minutes, or until tender.

Serves 4

# Harvest Vegetable Bake

1 onion, sliced

2 leeks, sliced

2 sticks celery, chopped

2 carrots, thinly sliced

1 red pepper, deseeded and sliced

500g mixed root vegetables, such as
  sweet potato, parsnip and turnip,
  cubed

2 cups mushrooms, sliced

2 cups canned chopped tomatoes

6 tablespoons dry cider

1 teaspoon dried thyme

1 teaspoon dried oregano

freshly ground black pepper

fresh herbs, such as basil and
  coriander, to garnish

1  Preheat the oven to 180°C. Place the onion, leeks, celery, carrots, pepper,
   cubed root vegetables and mushrooms in a large ovenproof casserole dish
   and mix well. Stir in the tomatoes, cider, thyme, oregano, and black pepper.

2  Cover and bake in the centre of the oven for 1–1½ hours, until the
   vegetables are cooked through and tender, stirring 1–2 times. Garnish with
   the fresh herbs.

Serves 4

Note: This satisfying vegetable dish is really cheap, especially in Autumn
when the ingredients are in season. Serve it with warm crusty bread.

# Red Onion, Courgette, and Tomato Pizza

1 tablespoon olive oil, plus extra for greasing

2 small red onions, sliced

1 yellow pepper, deseeded and sliced

2 small courgettes, sliced

1 clove garlic, crushed

2 cups whole-grain flour

2 teaspoons baking powder

3 tablespoons sunflower spread

½ cup low-fat milk

4 tablespoons tomato purée

1 tablespoon tomato paste

2 teaspoons dried mixed herbs

freshly ground black pepper

3 small plum tomatoes, sliced

½ cup low-fat aged Cheddar cheese, grated

fresh basil to garnish

1 Preheat the oven to 220°C. Heat the oil in a saucepan, then add the onions, pepper, courgettes and garlic and cook for 5 minutes or until softened, stirring occasionally. Set aside.

2 Place the flour and baking powder in a bowl, then rub in the sunflower spread. Stir in the milk to form a smooth dough and knead lightly.

3 Roll the dough out on a lightly floured surface to a circle about 4cm wide and place on a greased baking sheet. Mix together the tomato purée, tomato paste, mixed herbs and black pepper and spread over the dough. Top with the onion mixture.

4 Arrange the tomato slices on top and sprinkle with the Cheddar. Bake for 25–30 minutes, until the cheese is golden brown and bubbling. Garnish with fresh basil.

**Serves 4**

*Note: The red onions start to caramelise and become quite sweet while the pizza is cooking. If you don't have any mixed herbs, use dried oregano or marjoram instead.*

# Pumpkin and Artichoke Risotto

3 cups vegetable stock

1 cup white wine

1 tablespoon olive oil

1 onion, chopped

2 teaspoons ground cumin

½ teaspoon nutmeg

200g pumpkin, chopped

350g Arborio or risotto rice

440g canned artichoke hearts, drained and chopped

90g sun-dried tomatoes, chopped

2 tablespoons chopped fresh sage

freshly ground black pepper

30g grated Parmesan cheese

1  Place stock and wine in a saucepan and bring to the boil over a medium heat. Reduce heat and keep warm.

2  Heat oil in a saucepan over a medium heat, add onion, cumin and nutmeg and cook, stirring, for 3 minutes or until onion is soft. Add pumpkin and cook, stirring, for 3 minutes.

3  Add rice and cook, stirring, for 5 minutes. Pour 1 cup of hot stock mixture into rice and cook over a medium heat, stirring constantly, until stock is absorbed. Continue cooking in this way until all the stock is used and rice is tender.

4  Add artichokes, sun-dried tomatoes, sage and black pepper to taste to rice mixture. Mix gently and cook for 2 minutes or until heated through. Remove pan from heat, gently stir in Parmesan cheese and serve.

Serves 4

*Note: Arborio or risotto rice is traditionally used for making risottos. It absorbs liquid without becoming soft and it is this special quality that makes it so suitable for risottos. A risotto made in the traditional way, where liquid is added gradually as the rice cooks, takes 20–30 minutes to cook.*

# Roasted Vegetables with Mozzarella

2 carrots, cut into matchsticks

2 small waxy potatoes, sliced

salt and black pepper

1 tablespoon olive oil for brushing

1 red and 1 green pepper, each
  deseeded and cut into 8 pieces

1 aubergine, sliced

2 red onions, quartered

6 cloves garlic

1 ball mozzarella (about 145g), grated

### SAUCE

1 tablespoon olive oil

1 small onion, finely chopped

2 cloves garlic, crushed

2 cups canned chopped tomatoes

1 tablespoon tomato purée

1 teaspoon dried oregano

### SAUCE

1  Heat the oil in a heavy-based saucepan and cook the onion and garlic over
   a low heat for 5 minutes or until softened. Add the tomatoes, tomato purée
   and oregano. Bring to the boil, then reduce the heat and simmer, uncovered,
   for 20 minutes or until thickened.

### VEGETABLES

1  Preheat the oven to 230°C. Boil the carrots and potatoes in salted water for
   2 minutes or until softened slightly, then drain.

2  Meanwhile, brush 2 large baking sheets with oil. Divide the carrots,
   potatoes, peppers, aubergine, onions and garlic between the sheets,
   arranging them in a single layer on each. Brush with the oil, season, then
   roast for 20 minutes or until softened.

3  Spread the tomato sauce over the base of an ovenproof dish and arrange the
   vegetables on top. Sprinkle with the mozzarella and return to the oven for
   5 minutes or until the cheese has melted.

Serves 4

# Ratatouille in Fresh Tomato Sauce

3 tablespoons olive oil

2 cloves garlic, sliced

¼ teaspoon chilli flakes (optional)

2 red onions, sliced

1 aubergine, cut into 10mm cubes

2 courgettes, cut into 1cm cubes

1 fennel bulb, cut into 1cm cubes

1 yellow pepper, deseeded and
  cut into 10mm cubes

6 plum tomatoes, chopped

juice of ½ lemon

1 tablespoon soft light or dark brown
  sugar

1 teaspoon dried oregano

black pepper

1  Heat the oil in a large heavy-based saucepan, then add the garlic, chilli flakes (if using), onions, aubergine, courgettes and fennel. Stir well and cook, covered, stirring often, for 10 minutes, or until the vegetables have softened.

2  Add the pepper, tomatoes, lemon juice, sugar, oregano and black pepper to the onion mixture. Simmer, uncovered, for 10 minutes or until all the vegetables are tender, stirring occasionally.

**Serves 4**

*Note: Fennel gives this quick vegetable dish a delicate aniseed flavour, while the sugar adds to the natural sweetness of the vegetables. Serve with long-grain rice.*

# Baked Onions with Mushrooms and Pine Nuts

2 slices brown bread

4 large Spanish onions

2 tablespoon olive oil

2 cloves garlic, chopped

2 tablespoons pine nut kernels

2 cups mushrooms, chopped

4 tablespoons chopped fresh parsley

salt and black pepper

1  Preheat the oven to 160°C. Place the bread in the oven for 20 minutes or until it becomes crisp. Process in a food processor to make breadcrumbs.

2  Meanwhile, slice the tops and bases off the onions. Place in a saucepan, cover with water and bring to the boil. Cook for 10 minutes to soften. Drain and leave to cool for 20 minutes.

3  Increase the oven to 200°C. Cut out the middle of each onion, leaving the shell intact, and finely chop. Heat the oil, then fry the garlic and chopped onion for 5 minutes. Add the pine nuts and mushrooms and fry for a further 5 minutes. Remove from the heat, then mix in the breadcrumbs, parsley and seasoning.

4  Fill the onion shells with the mixture, then wrap each onion in foil, leaving the top open. Place on a baking sheet and cook for 40 minutes or until the onions are tender.

**Serves 4**

# Spicy Cauliflower with Garlic

2 slices brown bread

1 cauliflower, cut into florets

salt and black pepper

4 tablespoons olive oil

1 clove garlic, crushed

1 red chilli, finely chopped

8 black olives, pitted and halved

1 tablespoon capers

1 Preheat the oven to 160°C. Place the bread in the oven for 20 minutes or until it dries out and becomes crisp. Process in a food processor to make breadcrumbs.

2 Place the cauliflower in a saucepan, cover with boiling water and add a little salt. Return to the boil, simmer for 1 minute or until slightly softened, then drain well.

3 Heat the oil in a large, heavy-based frying pan. Add the garlic, chilli and cauliflower and fry for 3 minutes or until the cauliflower starts to brown. Add the olives, capers, breadcrumbs and seasoning. Fry for a further 1 minute or until the breadcrumbs soak up the oil and flavourings.

**Serves 4**

*Note: This method of cooking cauliflower comes from Italy. The fantastic combination of Mediterranean flavours will revolutionise your attitude towards this humble vegetable.*

# Orange-Glazed Cabbage

1 white cabbage, thinly sliced

**GLAZE**

juice of 2 oranges

2 tablespoons maple syrup

1 tablespoon olive oil

3 tablespoons marmalade

1 teaspoon salt

**GLAZE**

1   Place the orange juice, syrup, oil and marmalade in a large bowl and stir. Season, add the cabbage and mix to coat thoroughly.

**CABBAGE**

2   Preheat the oven 200°C. Remove the cabbage from the bowl, reserving the glaze, and spread it out on a large baking tray. Pour over ½ the reserved glaze and cook for 15 minutes. Remove from the oven, toss the cabbage gently, then pour over the rest of the glaze. Return to the oven and bake for a further 10 minutes or until the cabbage has turned dark brown at the edges.

Serves 4

*Note: The unusual but very simple glaze of marmalade, orange juice, and maple syrup gives the cabbage a lovely sweetness. This dish is particularly good with sausages.*

# Stir-Fry Broccoli with Almonds

2 carrots, cut into matchsticks

500g broccoli, cut into florets

2 teaspoons peanut oil

1 onion, sliced

1 clove garlic, crushed

2 teaspoons grated fresh ginger

2 teaspoons low salt soy sauce

2 tablespoons toasted almonds

1  Boil, steam or microwave carrots and broccoli until they just change colour. Drain and refresh under cold running water.

2  Heat oil in wok or frypan. Add onion, garlic and ginger and stir-fry for 4–5 minutes. Add carrots, broccoli and soy sauce, and stir-fry for 3–4 minutes longer, or until vegetables are heated through. Just prior to serving, toss through the almonds.

Serves 4

# Bean, Lentil and Aubergine Moussaka

½ cup continental lentils, rinsed and drained

1 aubergine, thinly sliced

2 tablespoons olive oil

2 leeks, sliced

2 sticks celery, chopped

2 cloves garlic, crushed

1 yellow pepper, deseeded and diced

2 cups canned chopped tomatoes

5 tablespoons dry white wine

2 tablespoons tomato paste

2 cups canned black-eye beans, drained and rinsed

2 teaspoons dried mixed herbs

freshly ground black pepper

1¼ cups low-fat plain yoghurt

2 medium eggs

2 tablespoons finely grated Parmesan cheese

fresh herbs, such as basil, to garnish

1 Add the lentils to a saucepan of boiling water, cover and simmer for 30 minutes or until tender. Drain, rinse, then drain again and set aside.

2 Preheat the oven to 180°C. Meanwhile, cook the aubergine slices in a saucepan of boiling water for 2 minutes. Drain, pat them dry with kitchen towels and set aside.

3 Heat the oil in a frying pan, add the leeks, celery, garlic and pepper and cook for 5 minutes or until slightly softened. Add the cooked lentils, tomatoes, wine, tomato paste, beans, mixed herbs and black pepper. Cover and bring to the boil, then simmer for 10 minutes or until the vegetables have softened.

4 Spoon ½ the bean and lentil mixture into a shallow ovenproof dish and layer over ½ the aubergine. Repeat. Mix together the yoghurt and eggs and pour over the top. Sprinkle over the Parmesan. Cook for 40 minutes or until golden brown and bubbling. Garnish with the fresh herbs.

**Serves 4**

*Note: Plenty of protein here for vegetarians. If you're in a hurry to get supper on the table, you can use canned ready-cooked lentils instead. Serve it with a green salad.*

# Sun-Dried Tomato and Cheese Puffs

6 tablespoons butter

1½ cups plain flour, sifted

½ teaspoon salt

4 medium eggs, beaten

1 cup Gruyère cheese, grated

## STUFFING

⅓ cup sun-dried tomatoes in oil, drained

4 tablespoons butter

## PUFFS

1 Preheat the oven to 220°C. Gently heat the butter and 1 cup of water in a large saucepan for 5 minutes, or until the butter has melted. Bring to the boil, then remove from the heat and stir in the flour and salt. Beat with a wooden spoon until mixture forms a smooth ball.

2 Gradually add the eggs, beating well, until the dough is shiny. Stir in the Gruyère. Place balls of dough (about 2 tablespoons each) onto a baking sheet and cook for 20 minutes or until risen and browned. Turn off the oven. Cut a slit in the top of each puff to let the steam escape. Return the puffs to the cooling oven for 5 minutes, then remove and cool for a further 5 minutes.

## STUFFING

1 Place the tomatoes and butter in a food processor and blend to a paste. Divide the paste between the puffs, packing it in with a teaspoon.

Makes 16

*Note: Gruyère combines beautifully with sun-dried tomatoes in these rich cheese puffs, which can be served at a drinks party or as a starter with some salad.*

# Banque Beans

300g fresh or frozen green beans

2 cloves garlic

1 teaspoon grated lemon rind

2 tablespoons lemon juice

1 tablespoon chopped parsley

freshly ground black pepper

1   Top and tail beans. String and slice if large or leave whole if using small round beans. Steam or cook in boiling water for 5 to 7 minutes or until just cooked and still bright green.

2   Drain beans and place in a serving dish. Crush, peel and finely chop garlic. Mix garlic, lemon rind and juice, parsley and freshly ground black pepper together. Pour over beans, toss to coat and serve immediately.

**Serves 4**

*Note: Plain steamed beans have to be one of the more boring vegetable experiences, so give yourself a flavour treat with this delicious variation.*

# desserts

# Grilled Honeyed Fruit with Vanilla Yoghurt

(see photograph on page 98)

3 tablespoons clear honey

2 tablespoons unsweetened apple juice

1 teaspoon ground mixed spice

1 ripe mango

1 small pineapple, peeled, cored and sliced

2 eating apples, peeled, cored and sliced

2 pears, peeled, cored and sliced

1¼ cup low-fat plain yoghurt

few drops of vanilla extract

1 Preheat the grill to high. In a bowl, mix together 2 tablespoons of the honey with the apple juice and mixed spice. Peel the mango and slice the flesh off the stone.

2 Cover the grill rack with foil and lay ½ the mango and the pineapple, apple, and pear slices on it. Drizzle over ½ the honeyed spice mixture. Grill for 10 minutes or until slightly softened, turning the fruit once. Keep it warm while you repeat with the remaining fruit and honey mixture.

3 Meanwhile, place the yoghurt in a bowl with the vanilla extract and the remaining honey, then mix well. Serve the fruit warm with the vanilla yoghurt mixture.

**Serves 4–6**

*Note: Fruit drizzled with honey and grilled until it just starts to brown is wonderful served warm with ice cream. But it's better still with vanilla yoghurt spooned over it.*

# Raspberry Yoghurt Ice

(see photograph opposite)

3 cups raspberries, defrosted if frozen

¼ cup caster sugar

1½ cups low-fat raspberry yoghurt

½ cup fat-free plain yoghurt

fresh mint and raspberries to decorate

1 Place the raspberries in a food processor and blend until smooth, or use a hand blender. Press the mixture through a sieve into a bowl, discarding the pips, then add the sugar and mix well.

2 Mix in the raspberry yoghurt and plain yoghurt. Pour the mixture into a shallow freezer container, cover and freeze for 2 hours. Meanwhile, put a large empty bowl into the refrigerator to chill.

3 Spoon the raspberry mixture into the chilled bowl and beat with a fork or whisk until smooth to break down the ice crystals. Return to the container, cover and freeze for a further 4 hours or until firm.

4 Transfer to the fridge for 30 minutes before serving to soften. Serve in scoops, decorated with the fresh mint and raspberries.

**Serves 4**

*Note: The unmistakable flavour of raspberries works really well in this tangy ice, but there's nothing to stop you using fresh strawberries and strawberry yoghurt instead.*

# Ricotta Torte with Fruit Compote

vegetable oil cooking spray

150g reduced fat plain (sweet) biscuits

2 tablespoons pecan nuts, toasted

3 tablespoons polyunsaturated spread or margarine, melted

1½ teaspoons powdered gelatin

zest and juice of 2 small oranges

zest and juice of 2 small lemons

1½ cups reduced fat ricotta cheese, well drained

¼ cup caster sugar

1 cup reduced fat sour cream

2 eggs, separated

## COMPOTE

½ cup dried figs

½ cup pitted prunes

½ cup dried apricots

½ cup dried cherries

2 tablespoons good quality Marsala

⅓ cup orange juice

zest of 1 orange

## TORTE

1　Spray a 20cm springform tin with canola spray and line the base with baking paper. Process the biscuits and nuts to fine crumbs. Add the spread or margarine and process for a few seconds to combine. Press firmly into the base of the tin. Chill for 30 minutes.

2　Dissolve the gelatin in a little hot water. Put the combined juices (but not the zest) in a small pot and heat gently. Add the gelatin. Remove from the heat and stir to dissolve the gelatin.

3　Beat the ricotta, sugar, sour cream, egg yolks and zest with an electric beater, then gradually pour in the gelatin mixture and beat slowly to combine.

4　Whisk the egg whites until stiff peaks form, fold 2–3 tablespoons of the egg whites into the ricotta mixture to lighten, then fold through the remaining whites, trying not to deflate the mix. Pour over the cookie base, cover and chill for at least 30 minutes. Slice into 10 portions.

## COMPOTE

1　Put the figs, prunes, apricots and cherries in a bowl and add the Marsala, orange juice and zest. Macerate in the refrigerator overnight. Serve the torte with fruit compote.

Serves 10

# Passion Fruit Soufflé

60g ricotta cheese

375ml passion fruit pulp

2 egg yolks

1 tablespoon orange-flavoured liqueur

75g caster sugar

6 egg whites

pinch cream of tartar

icing sugar, sifted

1  Place ricotta cheese, passion fruit pulp, egg yolks, liqueur and ½ the caster sugar in a bowl and beat for 5 minutes or until mixture is smooth.

2  Place egg whites and cream of tartar in a clean bowl and beat until soft peaks form. Gradually beat in remaining caster sugar until stiff peaks form.

3  Fold ⅓ of the egg white mixture the into passionfruit mixture, then fold in remaining egg white mixture.

4  Pour soufflé mixture into a greased 20cm soufflé dish and bake at 180°C for 20 minutes or until soufflé is well risen. Sprinkle with icing sugar and serve.

Serves 4–6

# Fruit Brûlée

440g canned unsweetened apple

4 tablespoons sultanas

1 teaspoon ground cinnamon

## YOGHURT TOPPING

100ml low-fat natural yoghurt

125g ricotta cheese

1 teaspoon vanilla essence

1½ tablespoon brown sugar

### FRUIT

1  Place apple, sultanas and cinnamon in a bowl and mix to combine. Divide mixture between four 250ml pie filling ramekins.

### YOGHURT TOPPING

1  To make topping, place yoghurt, ricotta cheese and vanilla essence in a food processor or blender and process until smooth. Spread topping over fruit, sprinkle with sugar and bake at 200°C for 25 minutes or until fruit is heated through and top is golden.

Serves 4

# Summer Fruit Compote with Vanilla Yoghurt

750g mixed summer berries, hulled or stalks removed and defrosted if frozen

½ cup port

¼ cup caster sugar

2 strips orange zest

juice of 1 orange

1 teaspoon ground apple spice

**VANILLA YOGHURT**

1 vanilla bean, split

1 cup plain yoghurt

1 tablespoon clear honey

**VANILLA YOGHURT**

1 Scrape the seeds from the vanilla bean into the yoghurt and stir in the honey. Cover and refrigerate while you make the compote.

**COMPOTE**

1 Put the berries into a saucepan with the port, sugar, orange zest and juice and the apple spice. Heat for 5–8 minutes, until the fruit is just softened. Remove from the heat and set aside for 15 minutes to cool slightly. Serve the warm compote with a spoonful of the vanilla yoghurt.

Serves 4

*Note: Thick vanilla yoghurt made with clear honey has a real Mediterranean flavour and tastes fabulous with this warm summer fruit compote. Serve with dessert biscuits.*

# Papaya Fruit Salad

½ papaya, cut in small squares

2 oranges, cut in segments

3 kiwifruit, sliced

small bunch sultana grapes

small bunch cordinial grapes

2 passion fruit, pulp only

1 banana, sliced

¼ pineapple, cut into small squares

1 punnet strawberries

6 mint leaves

juice of 1 lemon

3 tablespoons Grand Marnier (optional)

**1** Place all the cut fruit into a large glass bowl. Mix with hands.

**2** Pour lemon juice over the fruit salad, this will bring out the flavour of the pawpaw.

**3** As an optional extra taste delight, pour over Grand Marnier. Serve as a centre piece on a buffet table.

Serves 6

# Apple Tart Tatin

4 apples

2 tablespoons butter

½ cup sugar

½ teaspoon ground cloves

6 sheets filo pastry

½ cup soft wholemeal breadcrumbs

1 Peel apples if wished. Cut apples into quarters. Remove cores and slice thinly. Melt butter in a heavy-based frying pan with a metal handle. Add sugar and cook until mixture bubbles and sugar has melted.

2 Arrange apples in a cartwheel pattern over the base of the frying pan in the butter mixture. Sprinkle with cloves. Place a sheet of filo pastry on a board. Sprinkle with breadcrumbs. Repeat, finishing with a pastry layer. Cut pastry to the diameter of the frying pan. Place on top of apple. Cook on top of stove for 10 minutes.

3 Remove pan from stove and place in an 190°C oven for 10 minutes or until pastry is golden. Turn onto a serving plate and serve hot with a low-calories ice cream substitute.

**Serves 4**

*Note: Imagine never being able to have apple pie again all because you wanted to stay at a healthy weight. Well, get real! Life wasn't meant to be purgatory. Here's a lower-fat way to enjoy this comfort food.*

# Grilled Peaches with Raspberry Sauce

¼ cup ground almonds

1 egg white

1 teaspoon sugar

4 fresh peaches or canned peach halves

500g fresh or frozen raspberries

**1** Place almonds in a frying pan. Cook over a low heat, tossing all the time, until lightly golden. Remove from heat. Lightly beat egg white and sugar together until frothy. Mix in almonds. If using fresh peaches, cut peaches in half and remove stones.

**2** Bake at 180°C for 10 minutes. Place one teaspoon of almond mixture into the cavity of each peach half. Place one-third down from the grill element and grill until peaches are warm and almond mixture is lightly golden.

**3** Thaw raspberries if using frozen berries. Heat berries until almost boiling. Sieve to remove pips. Pour about quarter of a cup of raspberry puree onto four flat plates. Top with two peach halves and serve.

**Serves 4**

# index